FASTING
21 DAY DEVOTIONAL 2025

FASTING
21 DAY DEVOTIONAL 2025

Central Church

All Greek and Hebrew definitions come from the "Strong's Concordance" unless otherwise noted.

© 2024
Central Church

Printed in the United States of America
ISBN: 9798345188750

Table of Contents

Fasting Guide

Thank you for joining us this year for our progressive fast. You may ask yourself what a progressive fast is. A progressive fast is where we gradually take away items from our diet as we consecrate ourselves and take time to pray and ask what God would have for our church, families, and us, as individuals.

As we take certain things out the first week we will add to that week by week. By the end of the fast we will be in a complete surrender of flesh with our hearts and ears pointed towards heaven.

We understand many will do different variations of fasting and some may not be able to join us in fasting due to health restrictions. We completely understand and ask you to seek God in what He would want you to surrender. However, we are asking everyone to join us in prayer and devotion as we give God the first of our year and focus our attention on what He would want from us.

Week One: No bread and no dairy.

Week Two in addition to Week One: No caffeine and no sugar.
This includes sugar substitutes

Week Three in addition to Week One and Two: No meat. Ex. Fish, poultry, seafoods, and red meat.

Two Day Total Fast: Last two days of Week Three - No food.

This is only a guide that we as a church will follow. Please pray and seek God as to what dietary restrictions you choose to exclude or include during this fast.

This devotional guide is written by different members of Central Church under the direction of Pastors Darrell and Donna Allen.

Introduction

WOW!!

What an exciting time of year, New Year's is a time of new beginnings, a time of growth, renewal, and promise. It's also a time to refresh our spiritual life.

Sometimes we may become complacent in our relationship with the Lord, New Year's is a time to set our heart to run after Him.

Every year since the birth of Central Church, we have set aside the first twenty-one days as a season of First Fruits. A season of Prayer, Fasting, Giving, and Inviting. We believe that putting God first in all these areas can bring tremendous blessings within our lives. We also believe that doing these things helps establish healthy patterns of serving the Lord throughout the year.

I want to encourage us and our families to make the biblical practices of Prayer, Fasting, Giving, and Inviting a part of our everyday lifestyle and seriously set our hearts to run after God.

Although we do all these things throughout the year, this is a time when the main focus of our entire body is in unity and laser focused on the greater things that God has for us.

The next twenty-one days are extremely important, and powerful, and necessary to see the kind of spiritual advancement we are believing God for in this coming year. These practices will release the blessings and favor of God over our lives, families, businesses, our church, and our communities.

As we read the following pages, I pray that the Holy Spirit will draw us in and speak to us about this season of our life. Our desire is to help provide some basic guidelines along with daily words of encouragement and testimonies of what God has done in our lives, as well as plant some seeds of faith to motivate and equip us to pursue God through Prayer and Fasting.

As we venture into this next year, we believe that it will be the greatest year the church as a whole has ever seen. We believe that this year the church will see the greatest prophetic outpouring of God's Spirit and presence than we have ever seen before, more salvations, more healings, and more people set free and delivered.

Donna and I are so excited that you and your family have made the decision to embark on this journey together with us.

We look forward to hearing all the testimonies that, we believe, so many will have as a result of your obedience to the Lord.

Pastors Darrell and Donna Allen

Day 1: Spiritual Discipline Introduction

We open the first week of our fast focusing on spiritual disciplines. Discipline is limiting yourself for the purpose of a desired outcome to receive that is better for us.

As an example, if we want to reach our desired end state of being in physical shape, we need to limit our sleep habits and diet. The sole goal of spiritual discipline is to have a closer relationship with our Creator, our Savior, and our Comforter.

However, these do not have to involve limiting ourselves to reach our desired end goal of intimacy with Jesus.

Psalm 42:1-2, *"As the deer pants for the water brooks, so pants my soul for You, O God.*
2 My soul thirsts for God, for the living God. When shall I come and appear before God?"

When we come to the point where we just want to seek after God, and there is nothing that will stop us from drawing closer to God, then we are in a correct posture to receive what He wants for us in our lives. This desire comes from His goodness. We don't deserve His goodness, but He still chose to send His Son to die on the cross so that we could be in a relationship with Him.

Now, what are spiritual disciplines? Spiritual disciplines are practices we can put in place in our lives that promote spiritual growth and help us to grow closer to God. These examples are Biblical. Jesus practiced spiritual disciplines. This week we will cover the disciplines of Bible Study, Meditation, Submission, Service, Repentance, and Forgiveness.

- Bible Study: The study and application of God's Word.
- Meditation: Reflecting on God's Word.
- Submission: Submitting to Jesus and His Church.
- Service: Submitting our gifts to serve the needs of others.
- Repentance: Turning away from our sins.
- Forgiveness: Forgiving as we have been forgiven.

Some of these disciplines are done between us and God alone, and some are done corporately within the body of Christ. The goal is not to learn about these things and feel condemnation if there is any area that needs improvement. The goal this week is to learn ways to grow spiritually and to know Him in a deeper way.

Psalm 42:7, *"Deep calls unto deep at the noise of Your waterfalls; All Your waves and billows have gone over me."*

Peter once stepped out into deep water. He even walked on water with Jesus Christ. It was when he took his eyes off Jesus and started paying attention to the wind and waves that he sank. To step out into deep water we must keep our eyes on Jesus and not pay attention to what we see with our natural eyes. These actions are a way to grow our faith and build a deeper relationship with Him.

We have the choice. We can continue to be surface level Christians, where we treat salvation as enough, but sanctification requires too much change. We can make the choice that surface level Christianity is not enough for us, and we are going to answer the call to go deeper. This is where spiritual disciplines have their place within our lives. They are not just for pastors or leaders of the church. They are meant for Christians of every walk of life, from the newest convert to the most seasoned pastor, to practice so they can draw closer to God.

Our God is calling us to go deeper. To go deeper in His Word, our relationship with Him, with our families, and our communities. Our hope is that we will go into deeper water and be swallowed up by the Holy Spirit and our lives will be changed forever.

1. What is your impression of spiritual disciplines?

_____

_____

_____

_____

2. What is your response to God's goodness in your life?

_____

_____

_____

_____

3. How can you make practicing these spiritual disciplines a priority?

_____

_____

_____

_____

4. Of the spiritual disciplines listed; Bible study, meditation, submission, service, repentance, and forgiveness, which one do you feel you are the strongest in and why?

_____

_____

_____

_____

5. Of the spiritual disciplines listed; Bible study, meditation, submission, service, repentance, and forgiveness, which one do you feel you are the weakest in and why?

_____

_____

_____

_____

Personal Thoughts:

Day 2: Bible Study

Every parent can relate to the feeling of becoming a new father or mother. It's an exciting time, but it can be scary to know that we are responsible for this new life. It would be great if every child came with an owner's manual that would spell out exactly what their needs are and will be and exactly how to react in every situation.

That would be a useful book that each parent would pour over and know so that they can ensure that they are as good a parent as they could possibly be to their children.

Not to compare the Word of God with an owner's manual, but our Heavenly Father has given us His Word not just to tell us right from wrong, but for us to know Him. The Word of God is our connection to knowing His heart and the key to growing in intimacy with Him. The more we study the Bible and get the Word of God deep inside us, the more we allow the Word to transform us.

> **_Romans 12:2_**, _"And do not be conformed to this world, but be transformed by the renewing of your mind, that you may prove what is the good and acceptable and perfect will of God."_

We have an avenue to know our infinitely awesome God and yet sometimes we are guilty of disconnecting ourselves from God by not reading and studying His Word. We can be chasing after the heart of God in worship, prayer, and serving others but if we are not filling ourselves with His Truth then these activities can turn into religion.

> **_John 8:31-32_**, _"Then Jesus said to those Jews who believed Him, 'If you abide in My word, you are My disciples indeed._
> _32 And you shall know the truth, and the truth shall make you free.'"_

The word, "_If_," indicates this is a choice. We choose to either allow the truth of the Word of God to set us free, or to abide in the world and allow ourselves to get wrapped up in bondage. What choices can we make in our study habits that help us?

- **Pick a translation that makes sense to you**. Read a translation that you understand, and it will be easier to study. You might prefer to have a few translations on hand. You can use a Bible app that has many different translations to compare translations and decide which you like the most.
- **Commit to a regular time and place to study the Word**. This starts with a commitment to make regular time in your schedule. It doesn't have to be a set length, but it needs to be a time that works for you. The place you study at is important as well because you want to choose a place where you will not be distracted.
- **Find a plan to study (book of the Bible, person, theme, etc.)**. There are many different plans or methods you can utilize to study. You can start with a single book of the Bible or read through the Old or New Testament. You can study a person in the Bible. If you are dealing with a specific struggle it helps to study that topic. No matter how you plan to study, it is important to have a plan ahead of time but allow the Holy Spirit to lead you.
- **Pray for revelation**. When we invite the Holy Spirit to guide us into the fullness of His Word, He will respond. It is the reveled truth from the Word that leads to transformation within our lives. A wise man once said that he prays for two things when he studies the Word. First, show me Your Kingdom and secondly, show me Your Character.
- **Ask questions**. As you read, ask questions about what you are reading. Why did God include this in His Word? What is being communicated to us through this verse? How do we respond to what we are reading? There are many study Bibles, commentaries, concordances, and other resources to search out your answers. Find someone in the church that you can ask questions that you are having a hard time finding an answer to. Just don't stop asking questions and He won't stop answering.

These are just a few simple ideas to get you started in creating a habit of studying God's Word. Remember that this is not a check the box activity. Our reward is not simply gaining knowledge, but to gain intimacy with Him.

1. What do you currently do to study the Word of God?

_____

_____

_____

_____

2. What are some ways you want to improve in this area?

_____

_____

_____

_____

3. What is a regular time and place that you will commit to studying God's Word?

_____

_____

_____

_____

4. What type of plan works best for you to study the Word of God?

_____

_____

_____

_____

5. When you have questions while reading the Word of God, what are some ways you can find the answers?

_____

_____

_____

_____

Personal Thoughts:

Day 3: Meditation

Sometimes, meditation is not something that we associate with our Christian walk. We think about prayer, fasting and other things, but maybe not so much about meditation. Consider this verse:

> **Psalm 19:14**, *"Let the words of my mouth and the meditation of my heart be acceptable in Your sight, O Lord, my strength and my redeemer."*

The Psalmist is concerned that his words, and his thoughts and emotions, his heart, are acceptable to the Lord. The word here for "*heart*" in Hebrew is *leb* (Strong's #3820), and it means, "*the inner man, will, heart, understanding, mind, thinking, reflection, memory, conscience, emotions, passions, etc.*"

The Psalmist wants to make sure that what is happening in his unspoken life, his inner man, his emotions, thoughts, and passions honor the Lord. Everyone hears our words, but only us and God hear and know our inner thoughts and emotions. The Psalmist is concerned about this inner part of him being pleasing to God also.

What are we meditating on? What should our emotions and thoughts be focused on? Throughout the Psalms we find this phrase, "*I will meditate,*" and then different, but similar ideas, are given.

- "*On all Your work.*" Psalm 77:12
- "*On Your precepts.*" Psalm 119:15
- "*On Your wonderful works.*" Psalm 119:27
- "*On Your statutes.*" Psalm 119:48
- "*On Your word.*" Psalm 119:148

That's a good list. It must be understood that we all meditate. All of us have a thought life. It might be filled with worry, anxiety, all our problems. Sometimes our thoughts can overwhelm our mind and emotions. What we put into our minds is what we spend our time meditating and thinking about.

> **Psalm 119:11**, *"Your word I have hidden in my heart, that I might not sin against you."*

23

We must put His Word into our hearts. We must read and desire His Word. This is how we hide it in our hearts. Some people will say that reading and understanding the Bible is hard for them. This next verse can give us further insight.

Psalm 49:3, *"My mouth shall speak wisdom, and the meditation of my heart shall give understanding."*

What if we spent our time meditating and thinking about those verses or passages that are hard for us to understand? What if in our meditations we are also asking the Holy Spirit to help us understand?

Here is another place to meditate upon the things of the Lord. Mary, the mother of Jesus, has a whirlwind of a year. From an unmarried betrothed virgin, to having the Archangel Gabriel come and speak to her, getting pregnant by the Holy Spirit, traveling to Bethlehem, and giving birth Jesus in a stable, and being visited by shepherds. Let's agree that what Mary experienced had to be overwhelming, but Mary did something interesting.

Luke 2:19, *"But Mary kept all these things, and pondered them in her heart."*

She did not let all these experiences overcome her. She kept them in her heart, and she pondered them, she meditated about them. Even good and wondrous things can be powerful within our thoughts and emotions. Mary took time to sort them out carefully in her mind and spirit. Giving ourselves times of inward reflection can bring peace and clarity to us as we meditate on them before the Lord.

Our meditation can bring understanding and relevance to what has transpired in our lives, what His Word means to us, to know Him and to understand Him more. Our meditation can bring structure and peace to our experiences and what God is doing within our lives.

Perhaps there is another place of meditation that can have a high value within our lives. What if we took the time to meditate on His greatness and goodness?

Psalm 145:5, *"I will meditate on the glorious splendor of Your majesty, and on Your wondrous works."*

1. How much time do you spend meditating on the Lord, on His Word?

_____

_____

2. What is filling your mind? Are your thoughts consumed with the cares of life, with worry and anxiety?

_____

_____

_____

_____

3. Based upon Psalm 19:14, can you truly say that your thoughts and your meditations are acceptable to the Lord?

_____

_____

_____

_____

4. In our deepest thoughts, we stand alone with only God beside us. He knows our deepest emotions, fears, hopes, dreams, expectations, worries, and desires. How could you change your thoughts to bring them into alignment with Him in your life?

_____

_____

_____

_____

5. What might happen if you began to meditate on His wonderful works and goodness in your life? What if you turned your thoughts to remembering His great love for you? What good things has He done for you that you could meditate on today?

_____

_____

_____

_____

6. Have you hidden His Word within your life? Do you have a disciplined time to study the Word of God? It does not have to be hours each day, but it should be a regular habit. If not, what might this look like in your life?

_____

_____

_____

_____

7. Looking at Psalm 49:3, could you trust the Lord to help you understand His Word by meditating on the portions that you are unsure about? Are there any verses or passages now that you need further understanding?

_____

_____

_____

_____

8. Like Mary, sometimes our lives have multiple moving parts. These do not have to be bad or troublesome, but sometimes our lives do get busy and hectic. How could focusing your mind and pondering all the things that are happening give you peace and clarity? What might turning your attention mentally to the guiding of the Holy Spirit look like?

_____

_____

_____

_____

9. *Psalm 145:5, "I will meditate on the glorious splendor of Your majesty, and on Your wondrous works."* What if you spent some time meditating on just the wonder of our God? How could that affect your life today?

_____

_____

_____

_____

Personal Thoughts:

Day 4: Submission

There can never be true submission until we surrender all before Jesus. It is in this place that our love for the Father and the Son and the Holy Spirit is revealed.

John 14:15-16, *"If you love Me, keep My commandments. 16 And I will pray the Father, and He will give you another Helper that He may abide with you forever."*

The proof of our love for Him is our obedience, but there is something more. If we obey and submit, this allows Jesus to give us the Holy Spirit. We don't have access to the Holy Spirit unless we submit to His Lordship in our lives.

A disciplined life through submission and obedience is the call of the Master to His disciples. To be followers of Christ is to go where He goes…and to go as He goes. Jesus gave us the ultimate picture of submission when He bowed His will to the Father.

Matthew 26:39, *"He went a little farther and fell on His face, and prayed, saying, 'O My Father, if it is possible, let this cup pass from Me; nevertheless, not as I will, but as You will.'"*

This was the ultimate discipline. Jesus by His own admission could have called *"more than twelve legions of Angels"* (Matthew 26:53), but He did not. He bent His will to the will of His Father. In disciplined obedience, He submitted.

Discipline, submission, and obedience are not always our favorite words in the church. It is a place of protection and maturity that our church, Central Church, teaches and models obedience to the Word of God. It is a place of safety for us.

Often times we hear people talk about resisting the devil and he will flee from us. It sounds easy but not really. We do not have the power within ourselves to resist the devil. We must realize that there is more to this verse. It says,

James 4:7, *"Therefore submit to God. Resist the devil and he will flee from you."*

It is impossible for us to live a disciplined life before God without submission. The demoniac of the tombs who was possessed by a legion of demons had no ability to resist the devil. He had already lost that battle. When he saw Jesus getting out of that boat on the lake shore, he started running. Somehow, he knew if he could get to the feet of Jesus, that it was his only hope. Something new has happened, the presence of Jesus was near and there were not enough demons in hell to keep him from the feet of Jesus (Mark 5:1-20).

It has been said that advice we listen too, but pain we obey. There is some truth to that. Many times, we turn to Jesus in our pain, but perhaps not so much in the good times. He will meet whenever we come to Him, but a life of disciplined submission reveals true discipleship in our lives. It is when we pursue our Lord for who He is, and not what we need.

As we mature in the Lord, there is a deep desire to want more of Him that arises in us. That desire is to know Him, to walk in Him, and to live our lives for Him. This hunger for more of Him is proof of our growing and maturing in our faith. For this to happen we must learn to give up more of ourselves to have more of Him. This process requires discipline.

Paul teaches us that our lives can be compared to running a race and Jesus is the ultimate prize. We are not competing against others; the race is against ourselves. Paul mentions being *"temperate in all things,"* and to *"discipline my body and bring it into subjection,"* (I Corinthians 9:24-27).

A disciplined life will bow and submit to Jesus. Our minds and emotions will lie to us and if we listen to our flesh, we are pulled astray. There is another Scripture that we quote regarding spiritual authority. The weapons of our warfare are mighty, and they are. This passage is about our thoughts and emotions, casting down the strongholds and high things that draw us away. The crux of this passage is to take captive every thought to be obedient to Christ (II Corinthians 10:3-6).

Our hearts are deceitful (Jeremiah 17:9-10) and our minds are futile (Ephesians 4:17-20) if not submitted to the Lord. The greatest freedom is found in disciplined submission at the feet of Jesus! We must say, "Have Your way in my life Lord, I lay it all before You!"

1. Discipline, submission, and obedience are not always easy words for us to think about. Looking only at yourself, what areas of your life are already submitted to the Lord?

   _____

   _____

2. None of us are perfectly submitted, we all have struggles. What areas of your life are you still struggling with?

   _____

   _____

   _____

   _____

3. Jesus said that if we love Him, then we will obey His Word? The first question might be do we set aside time daily to spend in His Word? Do we need to make adjustments in our daily routine to make time for Him?

   _____

   _____

   _____

   _____

4. Jesus willingly chose to obey the Father even knowing that what He must go through was going to be very difficult. Jesus remains our perfect example for obedience. In the difficult choices of your life, how might you turn to Him and use His example of total obedience to submit our lives fully to God?

   _____

   _____

   _____

   _____

5. Sometimes the experiences of our life are There is healing and freedom for us, for all of us, in Jesus. Not even thousands of demons could keep the demoniac of the tombs from Jesus. Are there things that might keep you from coming and surrendering to Jesus?

_____

_____

_____

_____

6. We are in a season of prayer and fasting. There is something about a disciplined life. The New Year is often a time when we make new resolutions for ourselves. What new resolutions do you need to make with Jesus in your life?

_____

_____

_____

_____

7. Our thoughts and emotions are not trustworthy. Our emotions and intellect whisper all kinds of things to us, no devil needed. We make inner vows, like, "I am never going to do that again or go there again." What do your heart and emotions say to you?

_____

_____

_____

_____

8. What might happen in your life if you made a bold new decision and said to Jesus, "Have Your way in my life Lord, I lay it all before You!"

_____

_____

_____

_____

Personal Thoughts:

Day 5: Service

John 13:14-15, *"If I then, your Lord and Teacher, have washed your feet, you also ought to wash one another's feet.*
15 For I have given you an example, that you should do as I have done to you."

These Scriptures are the words of Jesus spoken while He was in the middle of what is one of the most meaningful acts found in all the Bible. Here we see Jesus washing the feet of His disciples, the ones who are following Him. He does this in an act of service and an act of love.

In washing the disciples,' feet Jesus leaves them two messages. The first is that Jesus loves them enough to deal with the dirt on their feet. The second being they should do the same for others. These are the same messages that He passes to us. At some point in our lives, Jesus has had to deal with our dirt, and He has cleansed us. He did this through the greatest act of service ever displayed, His crucifixion. As He has served us, He expects us to serve others. After all, we are still His disciples, just like those He was directly talking to in this passage. This means that we are to serve those around us.

Serving is the act of humbling oneself to benefit someone else. If you have ever been part of a foot washing, either the person washing or the person being washed, you know how humbling that is. Yet, Jesus still did it because it benefitted His disciples. This is the precedent Jesus sets for all His followers. This can be a challenging precedent to follow because it does not just deal with the action. This precedent also deals with the motive behind the action. If humbling yourself for the benefit of others is the requirement for Christ like serving, then serving to benefit yourself does not fit the requirement.

The culture we live in is conducive to a "me" centric lifestyle. The culture says, "If you want something, you can do whatever it takes to get it." Often, without noticing, we become susceptible to the current of the culture, and we fall into the trap of trying to make something happen. While our intentions appear to be good, our heart is deceptive (Jeremiah 17:9). This causes us to be doing good things with bad motives. Serving in this way is not the kind of serving Jesus is asking of us. Jesus asks for selfless serving.

He asks for selfless serving, because we are never more Christ like than when we serve from pure motives. Is that not the goal of our fast? To deny our flesh to be more like Jesus. Is that not the goal behind every spiritual discipline in our faith? Serving, with the right heart, is such an effective tool on our journey to be like Jesus.

Philippians 2:8, *"And being found in appearance as a man,*
He humbled Himself and became obedient to the point of
death, even the death of the cross."

Humility is both the prerequisite for, and result of, serving with a right heart. If you are going to serve with a right heart, it is going to start from a place of humility and it is going to end with an even greater humility. You get better at it the more you do it.

Serving starts like all disciplines; they are not fun to begin with (Hebrews 12:11). In the end, they produce the results we long to see in our lives, a more Christ like version of ourselves. Serving, with a pure heart, not only sets us up to be more like Christ, but is also the catalyst for a miracle.

Mark 2:3-4, *"Then they came to Him, bringing a paralytic*
who was carried by four men.
4 And when they could not come near Him because of the
crowd, they uncovered the roof where He was. So when
they had broken through, they let down the bed on
which the paralytic was lying.

This story here is a perfect example. Here four friends believing that their fifth and paralytic friend would be healed by Jesus. The four friends do not see a way to Jesus, so they made one. The story ends with the fifth friend walking out of the house Jesus was in.

What was the action tied to these friends' faith? It was pure hearted serving. They were humbling themselves with the motive to better their friend and bring him to Jesus. During this fast, may we see the miracles we are believing for and see ourselves become more like Jesus through the discipline of serving.

1. In John 13:14-15, we see Jesus tell His disciples that serving is an "*example*" He gives us to follow. How do you currently follow Jesus' example of serving in your life?

_____

_____

_____

_____

2. Since serving is a discipline in which we grow and become better at, where is one place you can take the opportunity to start or continue growing in serving?

_____

_____

_____

_____

3. When you serve, do you evaluate the motive behind serving? If so, are they often pure? Why or why not?

_____

_____

_____

_____

4. Are there places in your life where you have become susceptible to the "me" centric culture we live in? How can you practically give those places to Jesus?

_____

_____

_____

_____

5. As you grow in the discipline of serving, what do you desire to see change about yourself?

_____

_____

_____

_____

6. Is there a miracle that you are believing for you or someone else? If so, what is it?

_____

_____

_____

_____

7. What can you do to help serve other people that are either believing for the same miracle as you or to serve those who you are joining in faith for their miracle?

_____

_____

_____

_____

8. What are some action steps you can put into place to grow in serving over the rest of our fast?

_____

_____

_____

_____

Personal Thoughts:

Day 6: Repentance

Today we focus on repentance which is the same place Jesus started his ministry off with. The term repentance in the Old Testament means, *"to make a strong turning to a new course of action."* In the New Testament the meaning of the term implies, *"to change one's mind or purpose, always involving a change for the better."*

You may think that what you have done is too bad or that even if you repent it is too late. Take a few minutes to read about king Manasseh. In II Kings 21:1-16 Manasseh's sins are captured. He worshiped idols, rebuilt altars to false gods, practiced astrology, witchcraft, necromancy, among other demonic vile pursuits. In doing these things, he defiled the worship of the true God. He seduced the children of Israel into idolatry and wickedness. Manasseh was even involved in child sacrifice with his own son.

While that is a long list of sins that you may or may not identify with, you will probably in some form or fashion relate to this verse.

II Chronicles 33:10, "And the LORD spoke to Manasseh and his people, but they would not listen."

How many times is the Lord speaking to us and we're just not listening? Daily? Hourly? Maybe it's a willful sin that reveals to us that we need to turn it over to God. Maybe we are going through the motions, and we recognize that we have stopped listening to His voice. Regardless of where we find ourselves, it's time for repentance.

There is a military movement given to soldiers in formations that is a good picture of repentance. The command, **about face**, is given to a formation to turn the group from one direction to turn 180 degrees to the complete opposite direction.

When the person in command of the formation realizes the need to turn the group and march in the opposite direction, they will give the command **about face**. The people in the formation then execute the movement to turn from one direction, to facing 180 degrees the opposite direction. In the same way we must listen to the command of our Father when repentance is needed

41

and then be ready to turn away from our sins and behaviors. We have a choice when we hear the command of about face. If we are not listening or choose not to obey the commands, then we are disobedient and fall out of alignment which could possibly trip up ourselves or others around us.

We hear the promptings from the Holy Spirit and have a choice of listening, obeying, and acting on what we have heard. Repentance is really the other side of the coin from faith. We are turning away from our sin and putting our trust in Jesus, and there we find true forgiveness. True repentance leads us to life change.

The story of Manasseh recorded in II Kings was one of great sin. In II Chronicles his sins are written out for us again, but this time it captures something beautiful in verses 11-16. The Lord brought punishment upon him and in Manasseh's most desperate time in captivity he humbled himself and cried out to God. Manasseh, and his list of sins, didn't keep God from hearing his cries and delivering him back to his kingdom. Manasseh had an encounter with God where he knew beyond a doubt the Lord was God.

> **_II Chronicles 33:12-13_**, _"Now when he was in affliction, he implored the LORD his God, and humbled himself greatly before the God of his fathers,_
>
> _13 and prayed to Him; and He received his entreaty, heard his supplication, and brought him back to Jerusalem into his kingdom. Then Manasseh knew that the LORD was God."_

That is the God we serve. When we get our hearts in the right posture He will hear us, He will receive our prayers, and He will restore us. He has already sent His son to pay for our sins. In fact, if you read the genealogy of Jesus, you will find King Manasseh. God used this sinner and chose to bless his bloodline with the Messiah. It is time to humble ourselves and turn back toward His love.

1. Ask the Holy Spirit, what do you need to repent for?

_____

_____

_____

2. Are there sins your life that you think are too big for God to forgive?

_____

_____

_____

_____

3. Like Manasseh, are there times when the Lord is speaking, but you're just not listening?

_____

_____

_____

_____

4. How can you make repentance a daily part of your relationship with God?

_____

_____

_____

_____

Father God, I repent of the sins of _____. I ask you to forgive me, and I know that you do forgive me through the death of Jesus Christ on the cross. Jesus took those sins upon Himself and demonstrated His power over them when He rose from the grave. I choose this day to follow you and walk in your ways. I declare that Jesus is Lord of my life.

Personal Thoughts:

Day 7: Forgiveness

One of the most powerful things we can do as Christians is to forgive others. True forgiveness brings a new level of freedom to our hearts. It lifts the burden of carrying unforgiveness and can even cause sicknesses brought on by our unforgiveness to flee.

When Peter asks how many times he should forgive when a brother sinned against him, Jesus shared the solution.

Matthew 18:22, "Jesus said to him, 'I do not say to you, up to seven times, but up to seventy times seven.'"

Jesus goes on to share a parable about forgiveness. We will start at the end of the parable, where Jesus shares the consequences of unforgiveness. What happens to us when we choose unforgiveness?

Matthew 18:34-35, "And his master was angry, and delivered him to the torturers until he should pay all that was due to him.
35 So my heavenly Father also will do to you if each of you, from his heart, does not forgive his brother his trespasses."

When you do not forgive others then the enemy has the legal right to torture or oppress you. God will not bless unforgiveness and His divine protection from the enemy will not be upon you. Are you being tormented? This is probably an indication that you have unforgiveness in your life. Do you want to be free? The key is true forgiveness, from the heart.

As we work backwards in the passage, the next question we ask ourselves is why do we need to forgive others? Sometimes we have a legitimate reason for our unforgiveness, or we perceive that we have a reason when we judge others or decide to take offense to their actions. In either case, why are we held accountable for our unforgiveness?

Matthew 18:33, "Should you not also have had compassion on your fellow servant, just as I had pity on you?"

We forgive because He first forgave us. We are all sinners, and no one deserves God's forgiveness. However, God chose to have mercy on us and even sent His own Son to die on the cross so that we could receive His forgiveness. How can we receive the gift of His forgiveness through Jesus and then turn around and not extend forgiveness to our brothers and sisters?

That is the key to Jesus' parable. We have been forgiven of an eternal debt owed to God the Father. When we then turn around and hold debts against others it is hypocritical. We forgive on earth because He has forgiven eternally. Is it always easy to just forgive someone? No. People can be hurtful, either knowingly or unknowingly. That is why the enemy tries to convince you that it is impossible to forgive someone for what they have done to you.

To be clear, even if you have been abandoned, rejected, abused, traumatized, shamed, hated, or made to feel unworthy, you can still forgive. No matter the circumstance, you **can** forgive. Jesus took all those sins committed against you and paid the debt at the cross. Take them to the cross of Jesus in true forgiveness.

> **_Romans 12:17-19_**, _"Repay no one evil for evil. Have regard for good things in the sight of all men._
>
> _18 If it is possible, as much as depends on you, live peaceably with all men._
>
> _19 Beloved, do not avenge yourselves, but rather give place to wrath; for it is written, 'Vengeance is Mine, I will repay,' says the Lord."_

Your unforgiveness will not punish anyone but you. The Lord will judge and repay all our hurts. When someone hurts us the key to bringing them to repentance is not retaliation or resentment.

> **_Romans 12:21_**, _"Do not be overcome by evil, but overcome evil with good."_

When we truly forgive someone, this is what brings others to repentance. We don't forgive by trying to manipulate others to repent. That is not true forgiveness. We forgive and trust in God to work all things together for our good. In forgiveness we find freedom to move on and create lasting and wholesome relationships with others.

1. Are you tormented? If so, how?

_____

_____

_____

_____

2. Who do you need to forgive?

_____

_____

_____

_____

3. What do you need to forgive them for? (Be specific!)

_____

_____

_____

_____

4. Are you ready to forgive them from your heart?

_____

_____

_____

_____

5. Sometimes we say we have forgiven someone, but we still are tormented by the memories. Many times, this means we need to forgive on a deeper level, and often the enemy will continue tormenting us until we fully release the unforgiveness. Ask the Holy Spirit, is there anyone or anything you need to forgive on a deeper level?

_____

_____

_____

_____

Personal Thoughts:

Day 8: Territory Introduction

Territory is important to God. We know that He is the Creator. Everything that is, He is the Creator of it all, both seen and unseen. He owns everything, everywhere. God is an interactive God; He desires that we participate with Him in His creation and in His blessings and good gifts to us.

The territory that God gives us starts with what is in our hands relationally. When God saw that there was no helper for Adam, He created Eve. God intended that man, and woman would become one flesh (Genesis 2:23). It is the next verse that has even greater relevance for us to understand.

> *Genesis 2:24, "Therefore a man shall leave his father and mother and be joined to his wife, and they shall become one flesh."*

In effect, this becomes a new territory. A man leaves the covering of His parents, and joins with his wife and together, they become something new. What was not, now is, the two have become one. The man has a new responsibility to be the priest of his home and to cover and care for this new relational territory. Neither one of them is where they were, nor are they who they were. They were separate people, now they have become one. This is new territory in the physical and new territory in the spiritual.

Their territory expands if they have children. They both have new responsibilities before God to raise their children in the training and admonition of the Lord (Ephesians 6:4).

Our accountability before God territorially also changes in other dimensions as well. There are Old Testament promises that instruct us in this understanding. There is a promise that God gives to His people that is specifically tied to taking new territory, the Promised Land.

> *Deuteronomy 11:22-24, "For if you carefully keep all these commandments which I commanded you to do—to love the Lord your God, to walk in all His ways, and to hold fast to Him—*

23 then the Lord will drive out all these nations from before you, and you will dispossess greater and mightier nations than yourselves.

24 Every place on which the sole of your foot treads shall be yours: from the wilderness and Lebanon, from the river, the River Euphrates, even to the Western Sea, shall be your territory."

It is easy to say that this was an Old Testament promise, maybe it's not for us. We are not going to physically cross the Jordan River and take the land on the other side, but the principle has not changed.

Let's go back for a minute to the relationship territory that is created new in marriage, and new again with every child born to that family. Or perhaps you are not married, but God has given you something, perhaps many things that you might be responsible for. Do you have a job? Do you have a home, a neighborhood, a city, a county? Then there is territory in front of you that God expects you to be His witnesses in.

Do you have gifts, callings, ability, or anointings? What are you doing with them? The Lord has equipped you to accomplish His will to represent Him in every place that the sole of your foot treads. If you are a Christian, if you are in Christ, then where you go, He also goes, but how do we do that?

- For if you carefully keep all the commandments of God, His Word.
- If you love the Lord, your God.
- If you walk in His ways, His character.
- If you hold fast to Him, if you stand fast in faith.

What would happen in our lives, families, friendships, jobs, neighborhoods, and communities if we began to live our lives in ways that reflect these four principles? Something wonderful would happen, and God has attached a promise to our obedience in taking new territory. The passage says three significant words, *"then the Lord!"* If you go, He goes; if you obey Him, He gets involved!

1. Perhaps the idea of taking territory seems overwhelming. Start with what is right in front of you? What has the Lord given to you to be accountable for and to be His witness to?

_____

_____

_____

_____

2. If you are married, how is that new territory doing? The one that came into being when you and your spouse got married and became one flesh, something new before the Lord? If you are not married, how might you imagine being accountable before God if you get married?

_____

_____

_____

_____

3. Do you have children? If you do, then your territory expands again into their schools and activities. You encounter a new group of people, new territory. Are you taking this new territory? What does your witness look like in these places?

_____

_____

_____

_____

4. Ephesians 6:4 teaches us to raise our children in the training and admonition of the Lord? What does this look like in your house? Do you need to make any changes or adjustments in how you are raising your children?

_____

_____

_____

_____

5. What about the command to take the Promise Land in Deuteronomy 11:22-24. The Lord has a promise for you and your family as well. What does your Promised Land look like in the Lord? What territory are you praying for, or has He given you?

_____

_____

_____

_____

6. Take a minute and consider what other territories are in front of you. An easy way to identify your territory is to ask yourself, where do your feet go on a regular basis? That is your territory. Where is your territory?

_____

_____

_____

_____

7. Here are some questions that we all must ask ourselves. Are we carefully keeping the Word of God? Do we love God and does our life reflect that? Do we walk in His character of love and righteousness? Are we holding fast to Him in our faith? Are we giving Him the opportunity to show up in the territory that He has given us? What might our testimony be of "*then the Lord?*"

_____

_____

_____

_____

Personal Thoughts:

Day 9: Spouse

If we want to take new territory in our marriages, we first must make sure we have a solid foundation from which to build upon. Any foundation other than the solid rock of Christ will develop cracks from which the enemy will use to attack your marriage.

> *__Matthew 7:24-27__, "Therefore whoever hears these sayings of Mine, and does them, I will liken him to a wise man who built his house on the rock;*
>
> *25 and the rain descended, the floods came, and the winds blew and beat on that house; and it did not fall, for it was founded on the rock.*
>
> *26 But everyone who hears these sayings of mine, and does not do them, will be like a foolish man who built his house on the sand:*
>
> *27 and the rain descended, the floods came, and the winds blew and beat on that house; and it fell. And great was its fall."*

Our marriages need to have a foundation built upon Christ. Jesus discussed the issue of marriage when questioned by the Pharisees.

> *__Matthew 19:4-6__, "And He answered and said to them, 'Have you not read that He who made them at the beginning "made them male and female,"*
>
> *5 and said, "For this reason a man shall leave his father and mother and be joined to his wife, and the two shall become one flesh"?*
>
> *6 So then, they are no longer two but one flesh. Therefore what God has joined together, let not man separate."*

Did you catch the part where God is the One who joined the man and wife together? If you are married, then it is God's will for you to be married and stay married. The question then becomes, "How do we move our marriages forward?" Maybe you have had struggles in the past or are currently struggling as a couple now. Some of our marriages may just need some fine tuning.

Paul shares in his letter to the church in Ephesus wisdom

about marriage that we can use to strengthen our own marriages. In a marriage, we need to ensure that we remain pure for each other. No sexual immorality, bitterness, or sin can be allowed individually or as a couple.

> *Ephesians 5:25-27, "Husbands, love your wives, just as Christ also loved the church and gave Himself for her,*
> *26 that He might sanctify and cleanse her with the washing of water by the word,*
> *27 that He might present her to Himself a glorious church, not having spot or wrinkle or any such thing, but that she should be holy and without blemish."*

If you want to move forward in a marriage made in heaven, then each spouse must be holy. There should be no other person, other than your spouse, that shares the intimacy of the marriage. Emotional affairs and sexual affairs are equally destructive to our marriage. If those doors are open, then it is time to close them. Present yourself holy to your spouse and see how that can improve the quality of your marriage.

Next after holiness is selflessness.

> *Ephesians 5:28, "So husbands ought to love their own wives as their own bodies; he who loves his own wife loves himself."*

> *Ephesians 5:33, "Nevertheless let each one of you in particular so love his own wife as himself, and let the wife see that she respects her husband."*

No healthy person intends to hurt themselves. In a marriage when we are thinking only about ourselves and our needs, we lose sight of our partner's needs and then open the door to offense and strife. A healthy marriage is a selfless marriage where you prioritize your spouse's needs. Husbands, do you want to be respected by your wives? Meet her needs above your own. Wives, do you want to have your needs met? Respect your husbands.

Take new ground in your marriages. Purify yourself. Be holy and selfless in your marriage.

1. In what ways does your marriage show its foundation?

_____

_____

_____

_____

2. In what ways can you purify yourself for your spouse?

_____

_____

_____

_____

3. What are some ways you can be selfless in your marriage?

_____

_____

_____

_____

4. How can you show respect to your spouse?

_____

_____

_____

_____

5. Read Ephesians 5:22-24. Husbands, you have the responsibility to lead in marriage. Are you leading? Wives you have the responsibility to follow. Are you a good follower?

_____

_____

_____

_____

Personal Thoughts:

Day 10: Children

There they are. The people of God are standing in one large congregation just hours after He has delivered them from Egypt. They haven't even gotten to the Red Sea crossing yet. God begins to give them instructions regarding remembering this night of freedom and deliverance. He gives His people details on how to keep the Passover to remember forever that He is a God who can and will deliver. Then He says something else.

> *Exodus 13:8-9*, *"And you shall tell your son in that day, saying, 'This is done because of what the Lord did for me when I came up from Egypt.'*
>
> *9 It shall be as a sign to you on your hand and as a memorial between your eyes, that the Lord's law may be in your mouth; for with a strong hand the Lord has brought you out of Egypt."*

There are many reasons why we have children. There is one reason that is very important. The gift of children is the favor and promise of God for generational ministry in our families and lineage. Whether we realize it or not, we are teaching our children and are passing on information and experiences to them constantly. We can do this intentionally or unintentionally.

God tells us how to do this. *"And you shall tell your son in that day."* We are going to tell our sons and daughters many things. God is very specific here. "Why are we doing this Passover thing, Dad?" Why are you so serious about everything, "I mean it's just a lamb Mom."

"This is done because of what the Lord did for me when I came up from Egypt." This was the answer that was to be given. "Come here son and let me tell you why we are doing this today. You see, my God, our God, has brought me out of Egypt!"

We were not there thousands of years ago, but Egypt is a type of the world. If you are a Christian, then surely the Lord has brought you out of Egypt. Your children need to hear this. Your children need to know this. Not just this one time, they need to know it is a lifestyle before the Lord.

It is not just what you shall say to your children, it is how you demonstrate to them that you are a servant of the Most High God! In Exodus thirteen, verse eight are the words, but verse nine is the lifestyle we should be living before our wives, children, and family. *"It shall be as a sign to you on your hand and as a memorial between your eyes, that the Lord's law may be in your mouth; for with a strong hand the Lord has brought you out of Egypt."*

It is not just words; it is a life of obedience. When God created man and woman in His image and likeness, after blessing them, His first command was to *"be fruitful and multiply,"* (Genesis 1:28). This is the first instruction He gave to us. To be fruitful literally means to bear fruit. Psalm 127:3 says that children are the fruit of the wife's womb and a reward. A child, each of them, is a gift of not just our physical bodies but to us from God Himself. This same verse says that they are a *"heritage from the Lord."*

The word *"multiply"* means to grow and increase. God gave Abraham a promise over His Seed. Galatians 3:16 reminds us that the ultimate Seed of Abraham is Jesus Christ. This is what we are doing when we are *"fruitful and multiply."* We are called to raise a generational heritage of faithfulness to the Lord God in the earth. How? How can we do this? This can seem like a daunting task for just one couple leading their children.

> ***Exodus 13:9**, "It shall be as a sign to you on your hand and as a memorial between your eyes, that the Lord's law may be in your mouth; for with a strong hand the Lord has brought you out of Egypt."*

Moms and dads, grandfathers, and grandmothers, live a life that demonstrates the holiness and greatness of your Lord to your children and grandchildren. Let your faith be a sign on your hand and a memorial between your eyes. Let your thoughts and actions demonstrate your faith before your children. Let the praises and words of God be in your mouth when you speak to them.

Remind your children constantly of how God delivered you and your family out of Egypt. Tell them. Show them. Never stop!

1. In considering what God says to His people just hours after their deliverance, how does this affect you?

_____

_____

_____

_____

2. The gift of children to us is the favor and promise of God for generational ministry in our families and lineage. What does this look like in your family?

_____

_____

_____

_____

3. Has the Lord brought you out of Egypt? Do your children know what the Lord has done for you and how He did it?

_____

_____

_____

_____

4. Do the things that you tell your children about God line up with how you live your life? This is a very important question.

_____

_____

_____

_____

5. God's instruction to "*be fruitful and multiply*" concerns more than just physically having children. Have you really thought about your responsibility to generational ministry in your family?

_____

_____

_____

_____

6. God says that children are the reward and fruit of the wife's womb and are a heritage of the Lord (Psalm 127:3). Does this change your thinking about your children?

_____

_____

_____

_____

7. What is the sign that is in your hand? What is the memorial between your eyes? In the private realm of your home, when it is just you and your family, what are your actions, words and thoughts demonstrating to your children?

_____

_____

_____

_____

Personal Thoughts:

Day 11: Neighborhood

Acts 1:8, *"But you shall receive power when the Holy Spirit has come upon you; and you shall be witnesses to Me in Jerusalem, and in all Judea and Samaria and to the end of the earth."*

This verse is the last word that Jesus spoke to His disciples on the earth before His ascension to the right hand of the Father. His words echo the purpose of man that God gave to Adam. In Genesis 1:27-28a, God created man in His image and likeness and commissioned them take the territory of His creation. *"Then God blessed them, and said to them, 'Be fruitful and multiply; fill the earth and subdue it."* King David understood this:

Psalm 24:1, *"The earth is the Lord's and all its fullness, the world and those who dwell in it."*

God Himself proclaimed His love for His world, for His creation, in the sending of His Son to save and deliver us (John 3:16). Jesus reiterated this truth in His prayer to the Father that also included those of us who are in Him, His Church, today.

John 17:20-23, *"I do not pray for these alone, but also for those who will believe in Me through their word:*
21 that they all may be one, as You, Father, are in Me, and I in You; that they also may be one in Us, that the world may believe, that You sent Me.
22 And the glory which You gave Me I have given them, that they may be one just as we are One:
23 I in them, and You and Me; that they be made perfect in one, that the world may know that You have sent Me, and have loved them as You have loved Me."

This is a large task, showing the entire world that God has sent His Son for them. It may even seem overwhelming. There are two things of importance for us here. First, Jesus says that we are one with He and the Father and that He has given us a portion of His glory. Second, we have the power of the Holy Spirit. It is important that we understand who we are in Christ and through the Holy Spirit, who we are in the earth.

The gates of hell cannot prevail against the Church of the Lord

71

Jesus Christ based upon the revelation that He is the Christ of God (Matthew 16:13-19). We have been given great power and glory to be witnesses of Jesus Christ in the earth.

It starts in Jerusalem, or as we might say, in our neighborhoods with our neighbors. Now the question is, do we know our neighbors? If we do, do they know we are Christians? The answer is not found in what we have told them. Our first witness is what they see of us. When the lawnmower will not start, what is your reaction? Do the neighbors see us kicking and screaming at that inoperative hunk of metal? How about when they see us interacting with our children, our spouse, or our pets? This is the first witness that our neighbors notice.

If we invite them to church, would they be surprised to know that we go to church? These are fair questions. Neighbors notice one another. What are they seeing?

Jesus said that we receive power when the Holy Ghost come upon us and that we would be His "*witnesses.*" This is a strong word. In Greek, it is *martus*, (Strong's #G3144). The last portion of its definition is, "*|CI those who after his example have proved the strength and genuineness of their faith in Christ by undergoing a violent death.*" Many of us do not think of being martyred for Christ. What of this verse?

> **Romans 12:1**, "*I beseech you therefore, brethren, by the mercies of God, that you present your bodies a living sacrifice, holy, acceptable to God, which is your reasonable service.*"

What does our witness look like in our neighborhood if we are dying to ourselves and living a holy obedient life before God? Might our neighbors be more willing to know our Lord if they see Him lived out before them through us? Is the glory and majesty of the Almighty visible in our choices and lifestyle?

We have been granted intimate oneness with the Father and the Son. They have given us their glory and the power of the Holy Spirit. We may not travel the world, but our neighborhood is waiting for us to reveal the goodness and love of Jesus! "*And you shall be witnesses to Me in Jerusalem,*" in our neighborhoods.

1. The last words that Jesus said to His disciples on the earth was that they would receive power when the Holy Spirit had come upon them. Has the Holy Spirit come upon you? Is His power in your life? If not, what are you willing to do this year to change this?

_____

_____

_____

_____

2. Another part of Jesus' last words were about us being His witnesses. How does your life witness Jesus to those around you?

_____

_____

_____

_____

3. Psalm 24:1, "*The earth is the Lord's and all its fullness, the world and those who dwell in it.*" This would also mean that your neighborhood is the Lord's and all the people who live in it. Do your neighbors know that you are a Christian? How can you help them know that the Lord loves them?

_____

_____

_____

_____

4. It is a wondrous thought to know that Jesus has told us that those who believe in Him join in the oneness between the Father and the Son. He also said that He has given us His glory. The reason for this is that the world may believe in Him. What are you going to do with this oneness and glory?

_____

_____

_____

_____

5. What do your neighbors know about you? What have you exampled before them? Do you need to make changes?

_____

_____

_____

_____

6. Do your neighbors know that you are a Christian?

_____

_____

_____

_____

7. *Romans 12:1, "I beseech you therefore, brethren, by the mercies of God, that you present your bodies a living sacrifice, holy, acceptable to God, which is your reasonable service."* What does this look like in your life? How do you live your life as a living sacrifice, holy and acceptable to God?

_____

_____

_____

_____

Personal Thoughts:

Day 12: City

I Corinthians 1:2, *"To the church of God which is at Corinth, to those who are sanctified in Christ Jesus, called to be saints, with all who in every place call on the name of Jesus Christ our Lord, both theirs and ours.*

I Thessalonians 1:1a, *"Paul, Silvanus, and Timothy, to the church of the Thessalonians in God the Father and the Lord Jesus Christ."*

There are some important things to consider here. Paul is writing his letters to a church in a city. It was a city church. It was the church at Corinth, or the church in Thessalonica. One church, in one city, representing one Lord and one God in that location. This is how God takes territory. He raises up His people in a location. To accomplish this, He calls people to specific places to accomplish His purpose in specific territories.

Our obedience is tied to not only the gifts of our calling, but also to the location of our calling. We would have never heard of Abraham if he had not left his country, his family and his father's house (Genesis 12:1).

Many churches start for many different reasons. Not all these reasons have anything to do with God. Many churches were started out of anger or offense, because people wouldn't submit or obey in other places. They got mad, got up, stole some sheep, and started doing their own thing as a "church." These never end well.

The Lord does not plant churches, He plants gifting and anointing in specific locations for His purpose. Central Church is called to this location. Our pastors were raised up in this town, in this region, to take the city and the surrounding territories. Central Church is called to touch the surrounding areas and influence whole world, but it starts with what we do in the location where God has placed us.

How do we do that? How do individuals and families join with a local church to accomplish God's purpose in Covington, Newton County and the surrounding region? It takes corporate obedience to the vision and call of God.

To be a part of this we must submit our lives and families to a vision larger than ourselves. If we are only going to a church because of the things we need, we will never take any territory for the Lord. There is certainly a place to come and get healed, saved, delivered, and set free. Come one and come all to the Church of the Lord Jesus Christ! However, there is more, so much more. For a church to take territory for the Kingdom of God:

1. There must be called, gifted, anointed, and visionary pastors. God raises up men and women in territories. God has raised up our pastors, Darrell and Donna Allen in Covington, for this purpose.

2. There must be the presence of other called pastors and leaders submitted to the vision of the called pastors to facilitate the work of the ministry.

3. There must be a congregation, a people submitted to the vision that God has placed in the church to take the territory. Paul speaks to this when he says, "*to those who are sanctified in Christ Jesus, called to be saints, with all who in every place call on the name of Jesus Christ our Lord.*"

This is the congregation that God calls to take territory. A sanctified people, a holy people, a people who begin to lift up the vision and purpose of God and begin to call upon the name of Jesus in that territory.

This is what a church taking territory looks like. A people in one purpose, submitted to, and following the anointed vision of called leaders before God. Pastors who are submitted to God, who teach the Word of God in its fullness and authority.

Then something wonderful begins to happen, God's people begin to arise and shine! Darkness is pushed back as the Church, the people of God, begin to manifest the glory and majesty of God in a location, in a territory.

Romans 8:19, "*For the earnest expectation of the creation eagerly waits for the revealing of the sons of God.*"

Let us take Covington, Newton County, and the surrounding region by being the revealed sons and daughters of God! Arise and shine, Church! Till all the earth is filled with His glory!

1. How do you view your church? Do you believe that Central Church is called to take territory for God?

_____

_____

_____

_____

2. What brought you to this church? How did God lead you to Central Church?

_____

_____

_____

_____

3. In Ephesians 4:16 the Word says that His church is "*fitly joined together.*" This means that the Lord does this. Have you ever thought about a specific location as being a part of your obedience to the Lord?

_____

_____

_____

_____

4. What does it mean to you in considering that God does not plant churches, He plants gifting and anointing in specific locations for His purpose?

_____

_____

_____

_____

5. Our church's mission statement is to "*Lead people into a life changing relationship with Jesus Christ.*" How do you being a member of Central Church align with this mission?

_____

_____

_____

_____

6. In 2022, our South Campus was birthed, and in 2023 we planted a church in Cambodia, and now we are now **one church in three locations**. Our pastors have told us that their vision includes further growth and more locations. What do you think that looks like to you and your family?

_____
_____
_____
_____

7. Speaking to the church at Corinth, Paul addresses the congregation as "*to those who are sanctified in Christ Jesus, called to be saints, with all who in every place call on the name of Jesus Christ our Lord.*" We are members of Central Church, and we represent the Body of Christ in the earth, in Covington. How does your life fit into this description?

_____
_____
_____
_____

8. *Romans 8:19, "For the earnest expectation of the creation eagerly waits for the revealing of the sons of God."* What does this look like for you? Are you a revealed son or daughter of God in your church, in Covington, in Newton County, in the earth?

_____
_____
_____
_____

Personal Thoughts:

Day 13: Country

__Acts 1:8__, "But you shall receive power when the Holy Spirit has come upon you; and you shall be witnesses to Me in Jerusalem, and in all Judea and Samaria and to the end of the earth."

We have come to understand that it is first Jerusalem, Judea, Samaria and then all the rest of the earth. Samaria is an interesting place on this list. Jerusalem represents our close environment, our neighborhoods. Judea is our City. Samaria represents our country. For us this would mean America.

There is an aspect of Christianity in America that we must carefully understand. There has been a blending of the two that is not totally true. God has raised up America and given us freedoms to allow us to represent Him in ways that most other nations do not have. That is a gift of God to us. We cannot afford to blur the line. Being an American is not the same as being Christian. The Church is called to be the bride of Christ in the earth, and being Americans allows us freedoms to accomplish this.

However, both our nation and our faith are under assault. Our culture is in disarray. We are seeing things happen in our country that most of us probably could not have imagined just a few years ago. The mistrust of our government and news outlets is rampant. Sin and crime have free reign. The people are cynical when considering our elected leaders and perhaps even the elections themselves. What are we as Christians to do?

Some theologies just say love everybody, everywhere, all the time and it's all ok, but where is the righteous standard of the Word of God? According to the Word of God, everything is not ok, everywhere, all the time. This is the cue for the Church of the Lord Jesus Christ to arise in our neighborhoods, cities, and country. We as individual Christians and as His Church have a calling, a responsibility to live His righteous standard in our nation, in the earth.

Now we come back to Acts 1:8, the last words of Jesus on the earth to His disciples. He did not tell them to just go to church twice a week, (or maybe just once a week.) He told them to be the Church, and how do we do that? We are each just one person, one family, in a small city. If that is our only vantage point, then maybe not so much. There is something else, there is the promise of power.

The word for "*power*" in Acts 1:8 is *dunamis*, (Strong's, #G1411). It means, "*strength, power, ability, inherent power for performing miracles, moral power, the excellence of soul.*" We might wonder how we can get this power, but Jesus has already given us the solution. The answer is a Person, and that Person is the Holy Spirit.

We want to change our nation, but how do we do that? "*You shall receive power when the Holy Spirit has come upon you.*" Step one, the Holy Spirit comes upon you. It must start here in each of us individually. This is best understood as a relational place. The inference in Greek for this is that the Holy Spirit has descended on us and is operating through us. However, both require submission and obedience.

The Holy Spirit is not going to do this if someone is an unbeliever or unwilling. He is not going to make you do anything. You must invite Him, and you must submit to His guidance in your life, but if you do, there is that promise of power. "*You shall receive power when the Holy Spirit has come upon you.*"

This is how we take our country, as individuals, in the power of the Holy Spirit, becoming one in the Church for His corporate purpose. We can't change America by ourselves, but when the Holy Spirit comes upon us, comes upon us, all things become possible.

There is also the promise of purpose, the reason for the infinite power of the Holy Spirit within us. "*You shall be witnesses to Me.*" This is the promise of purpose in our lives. Do we realize that the changing of our nation starts with the changing of our hearts in submission to the Holy Spirit, to be His witnesses? Oh Church, we have work to do!

1. How do you view your country? How do you view America? Would you consider America to be a Christian nation?

_____

_____

_____

_____

2. Have you thought of your Christianity in terms of being an American?

_____

_____

_____

_____

3. If a change of focus is needed, how do you think about the Church of Jesus Christ in America?

_____

_____

_____

_____

4. What responsibility do you have toward your country as a Christian? Do you have places of influence?

_____

_____

_____

_____

5. God is love. He is also righteous. How could you love people in His love and yet hold a righteous standard according to His Word?

_____

_____

_____

_____

6. It will take a corporate witness to change our nation. This means our church and other churches being His witnesses. How healthy is your relationship with your church? Do you need to make any changes?

_____

_____

_____

_____

7. Has the Holy Spirit come upon you? Has your life been changed by your submitted relationship with Him?

_____

_____

_____

_____

8. Do you have the Holy Spirit's power to be witnesses of Christ? What does this obedience look like? What more could you do?

_____

_____

_____

_____

Personal Thoughts:

Day 14: Missions

In Acts 1:8, Jesus says that we would be His witnesses to the ends of the earth. While that sounds vague, the point is that His Church would be His witnesses to the whole world. Most of us as Christians and as members our church, will probably never spend our lives in the mission field of some far-flung country.

There are other ways to get involved. Matthew 24 is not always a happy chapter to read. There are numerous interpretations about this chapter, what will happen, when it will happen, how it will happen. There are some straightforward truths found there. Let's consider one of them.

> *Matthew 24:13-14*, *"But he who endures to the end will be saved.*
>
> *14 And this gospel of the kingdom will be preached in all the world as a witness to all the nations, and then the end will come."*

It is important when considering this passage that we always include verse thirteen. How can we be a witness if we do not endure? We present no witness to anything if we quit or give up. However, it is verse fourteen that captures our attention. There is a very specific promise attached to this Scripture.

Remember, we are still talking about missions to the ends of the earth. This verse tells us three things, and then the promise. We will find ourselves in this verse. We can participate in the far-flung mission field, it's a sure thing if we are willing.

1. The message that is preached in the gospel of the kingdom. Now we are used to hearing about the gospel, the good news, but what about the gospel of the kingdom? They are sort of the same thing. The word for *"kingdom"* is *basileia*, (Strong's, #G932). The definition of this word deals with the authority of God and His right to exert power and influence within His realm. His realm is the whole world, all of creation.

   The word for *"gospel"* is *euaggelion*, (Strong's #G2098). It does mean good news and good tidings. However, it also says, *"the glad tidings of the kingdom of God soon to be set up, and subsequently also of Jesus the Messiah, the founder of this kingdom.*" It is good news that Jesus is our Savior. It is also good news that He is the King of God's Kingdom. His power and His rule are absolute over all His creation.

2. The *"gospel of the kingdom will be preached in all the world."* Now we are talking about the mission field, all of it. That mission field also includes the street that you live on! You do have a mission field!

3. It will be preached *"as a witness to all the nations."* Consider that word *"witness."* This is a demonstration, a living testimony, not just telling someone about the Lord. It is a witness, a life lived out in service and obedience to God. A life that is steadfast and endures to the end.

We can participate in the mission field with our financial giving and with our prayers. We should do these things, and more. There is a mission field in our homes, families, streets, jobs, and cities. We have an opportunity to witness our King in the earth.

It takes the whole Church throughout the world to reach all nations and all the earth. Not everyone will go to Africa, or China or Cambodia. Not everyone will go to your street, but you can. Before a church can touch the world, it first must touch its city. Central Church is doing both. We are touching our city, county, and region. We are also touching the nations.

As members of the Church, we participate in all of that as we volunteer, serve, give tithes and offerings, pray and intercede for the world and for the nations. Not to forget, all missions start in our homes and families. Our witness starts there, but it does not end there. Our witness goes right down the middle of our street to all the nations to the ends of the earth.

The last part is a promise. It is the purpose of God that His glory and His witness fill the earth, *"and then the end will come."* We may not know when, or exactly how, but we have work to do.

__Matthew 9:37__, "Therefore pray the Lord of the harvest to send out laborers into His harvest."

90

1. What do you think of when you think of the mission field?

_____

_____

_____

_____

2. Part of our witness is enduring. Jesus said that "*he who endures to the end will be saved.*" What does enduring look like in your life?

_____

_____

_____

_____

3. Are there areas in your life that you are not doing a good job of enduring? What changes might you need to make?

_____

_____

_____

_____

4. Matthew 24:14 says that it is the "*gospel of the kingdom*" that is preached. What do you think this means?

_____

_____

_____

_____

5. This gospel will be preached in all the world. What does this look like to you? Have you ever been on a mission trip or spent time in the mission field? What can you do to participate in this purpose?

_____

_____

_____

_____

6. What does it mean to be a witness? Is it the things we say or do or both? Is it something different?

_____

_____

_____

_____

7. It seems that this is very important to the Lord. He has specified the message and the location. His kingdom is to be witnessed in all the earth. Jesus said that the fields are already white with the harvest. He is looking for laborers to go into the fields as His witnesses. How do we individually and as a church accomplish this?

_____

_____

_____

_____

Personal Thoughts:

Day 15: Spiritual Warfare Introduction

Spiritual warfare is a big topic. We might think of that war in heaven when Satan dared to challenge God! That was a very short war. The strong power of the Almighty was instantly victorious. That name, the Almighty, sums up the infinite power of our God.

We know there is a kingdom of darkness. We know that Satan *"walks about like a roaring lion, seeking whom he may devour,"* (I Peter 5:8). Just as an aside, please remember that he is only *"like"* a lion. True spiritual warfare begins with a few truths.

- Jesus is **the** Lion! He is the Lion of the tribe of Judah (Revelation 5:5).
- Jesus holds all power and authority and has conquered the enemy! Jesus humiliated Satan making on open spectacle of him (Colossians 2:15).

Our understanding of spiritual authority must not be that we are on the side that is winning. We are on the side that has **already** won! We war out of the finished work of the victorious Christ. Jesus reigns as King over all the demonic principalities and powers, and He has given this power to His Church, (Ephesians 1:19-23)! We see deliverance and healing take place often at Central Church, at the altar, in prayer rooms, and other places.

There is another way to do spiritual warfare that perhaps we might not think about. Spiritual warfare happens every time the kingdom of darkness meets the Kingdom of God. We are taught about the whole armor of God from Ephesians 6, and we must be prepared and properly arrayed with our spiritual weapons and armor. Let's consider a slight shift in our thinking.

John 10:10-11, *"The thief does not come except to steal, and to kill, and to destroy. I have come that they may have life, and that they may have it more abundantly.*
11 I am the good Shepherd. The good Shepherd gives His life for the sheep."

The enemy comes to steal, kill, and destroy. Jesus comes out to do battle with the adversary in full armor and a great sword, as a *"good Shepherd?"* What? The enemy is stealing and killing and destroying, and Jesus is the "*good Shepherd?*" That seems about right. A young shepherd boy named David slew the giant Goliath.

There might be more to this picture of the "*good Shepherd.*" The Greek word for "*good*" is *kalos*, (Strong's, #G2570). It has a long definition, but the highlights are "*excellent in nature and characteristics, genuine, purity of heart and life, morally good, conferring honor, affecting the mind agreeably, comforting and confirming.*"

Let's go to battle and start doing spiritual warfare. Let's make sure first that we are in Christ! Let's have all the pieces of our armor on. Let's keep our sword sharp by use and discipline in the Word of God, and let's follow the "*good Shepherd*" into battle. Oh yes, the "*good Shepherd*" knows how to fight, for He reigns as the victorious Lord of glory. Ready? Here we go to the front lines!

The enemy comes to steal. What can we do in the service and character of the "*good Shepherd?*" We begin to give back what the enemy has stolen. We remind them that the Lord can return all things that the locusts have stolen (Joel 2:25). Where he has stolen a person's worth and purpose, we give back dignity. Where he has given chaos, we give back the peace of Christ.

The enemy comes to kill. In the service of the Master, we speak and give life! Only Jesus can raise the dead, but we can help unwrap the grave clothes of the ones who are following Lazarus out of the tomb, (John 11:1-44). We give life to those that still have the smell of death clinging to them.

The enemy comes to destroy. In the service of the Risen Lord, we rebuild. Where he has destroyed hope, we return purpose. Where he has destroyed identity, we reveal the image of the Lord that is available to the redeemed. Where he has laid waste, we are called to restore. "*Those from among you shall build the old waste places; You shall raise up the foundation of many generations; and you shall be called the Repairer of the Breach,*" (Isaiah 58:12).

Ready yourselves, the Church is called to war! The "*good Shepherd*" calls us to follow Him and return, revive, and restore!

1. When you think of spiritual warfare, what comes to your mind?

_____

_____

_____

_____

2. Can you see yourself on the front lines doing spiritual warfare?

_____

_____

_____

_____

3. Are we giving Satan too much credit in our lives? He is roaring, but are we listening? What lies has he roared in your life?

_____

_____

_____

_____

4. Satan is only "*like*" a lion. The true Lion is Jesus Christ. Does this change anything in your thinking about spiritual warfare?

_____

_____

_____

_____

5. Our understanding of spiritual authority cannot be that we are on the side that is winning. We are on the side that has **already** won! We war out of the finished work of the victorious Christ. What could this understanding mean in your life?

_____

_____

_____

_____

6. Do you war the enemy out of the character of the *"good Shepherd?"* Do you need to make changes?

_____
_____
_____
_____

7. The enemy comes to steal, but the *"good Shepherd"* gives back. How can you do this like Jesus?

_____
_____
_____
_____

8. The enemy comes to kill, but the *"good Shepherd"* gives life. How can you do this like Jesus?

_____
_____
_____
_____

9. The enemy comes to destroy, but the *"good Shepherd"* restores and makes new. How can you do this like Jesus?

_____
_____
_____
_____

Personal Thoughts:

Day 16: Communion

When we think of communion our minds quickly go to thoughts of oyster crackers and grape juice, or the plastic wafer under the impossible to open wrapper. Communion is so much more. The word communion itself calls for an intimate exchange of emotions, thoughts, and feelings.

> *I Corinthians 11:23-26, "For I received from the Lord that which I also delivered to you: that the Lord Jesus on the same night in which He was betrayed took bread;*
> *24 and when He had given thanks, He broke it and said, 'Take, eat; this is My body which is broken for you; do this in remembrance of Me.'*
> *25 In the same manner He also took the cup after supper, saying, 'This cup is the new covenant in My blood. This do, as often as you drink it, in remembrance of Me.'*
> *26 For as often as you eat this bread and drink this cup, you proclaim the Lord's death till He comes."*

Paul writes from a place of communion and surrender. When we take communion, it is not about the act but about the communication. First, we are allowing God to see us and through us all the while exchanging what we lack for what He did on the cross. We are reminding ourselves and reminding the enemy that we are in relationship with Christ. The old man is dead (II Corinthians 5:17). It was broken on the cross. It was taken by each wound, it was absorbed by each bruise and through His stripes, **we have healing** (Isaiah 53:5).

Healing words that bring us back to the cross to remind ourselves that it is finished (John 19:30). When we take communion, it is first a place of repentance: *"Lord forgive me if I have been out of communication with you. Forgive me of any sin knowingly or unknowingly that has taken my focus off you."*

Secondly, we remind ourselves that because we've been forgiven, we must forgive (Ephesians 4:32). He was wounded, so we don't have to be. He was bruised, so we don't have to be. He was whipped, so we don't have to be. He died, so we can have

Eternal Life.

Third, we make it a point of celebration: we are partaking of the Living Bread, we are coming alive with Him (John 10:10). The bread was broken so we could be whole. Jesus' Blood was spilled so that we could be His. The Blood is the source of the covenant (Mark 14:24). The Blood does not only wash us it grafts us into the family of God. It's the DNA and the source of life (Leviticus 17:11). It is now our identity. It is who we are. We are children of God.

Let us now celebrate because we are His beloved and He is ours. We celebrate because the work is finished. We celebrate because we serve a God who is alive and still on the throne (Revelation 1:18, 5:13). We celebrate, because greater is He that lives in us than he that lives in the world (I John 4:4). We are in communion with Him. Better yet, we are part of a family founded in the name of Jesus where with all hell trembles. We are **His** (Acts 17:28).

1. What does communion mean to you?

_____

_____

_____

_____

2. What areas are you in need of healing in?

_____

_____

_____

_____

3. In what part of your life do you need forgiveness or to forgive?

_____

_____

_____

_____

4. Take time to celebrate. What has God done for you?

_____

_____

_____

_____

5. Take time to reflect. What do you need God to do in this season?

_____

_____

_____

_____

6. Where in your life do you need to surrender?

_____

_____

_____

_____

Personal Thoughts:

Day 17: Prayer

In Matthew chapter six, Jesus not only gives us a model, a pattern for prayer, but the parameters of how we should approach prayer. Jesus gives two significant things that we should not do.

1. "*And when you pray, **you shall not be like** the hypocrites; For they love to pray standing in the synagogues and on the corners of the streets, that they may be seen by men,*" (Matthew 6:5-6). The word for "*hypocrites*" is *hupokrites*, (Strong's, #G5273). The definition is, "*an actor, stage player, pretender.*" This is selfish, prideful prayer. This prayer is not for God but for us, it is not directed to God but to the audience watching us.

   Jesus tells us instead to go into our rooms, shut the door and pray to the Father in that secret place. This is the place of prayer, intimacy with only you and the Father (Matthew 6:6).

2. "*And when you pray, **do not use vain repetitions** as the heathen do.*" The subject here is "*a heathen, a pagan, ones who are alien to the worship of the true God,*" (*ethnikos*, Strong's, #G1482).

   Instead, Jesus instructs us to remember that when we ask of the Father, He already knows what we have need of (Matthew 6:8).

This is when we immediately start talking about the Lord's Prayer and the Lord goes there next. Perhaps it might be important that we just stay in this place and consider the two individuals that Jesus has brought up. He gives no names, no identifiers, just a hypocrite and a heathen, and this should give us pause.

Are we willing to ask ourselves a difficult question? Is there any portion of hypocrisy in our attempts to follow Christ? Is there any part of us that secretly wants to be noticed for what we do? If we are honest with ourselves, that answer is probably yes to some extent. This is the fight against our flesh. This taps into our human need to be wanted, accepted, valued, and appreciated. We must be vigilant in our witness that we do not begin to stand in any level of hypocrisy. It takes surrender and discipline to put the Father first in all things; both privately and publicly.

The second person is the heathen. Notice the phrase in Matthew 6:7. The heathen was using "*vain repetitions*," in his prayer. In Greek, the phrase is one word, *battologeo* (Strong's #G945). It means, "*to stammer, to repeat the same things over and over, to use many idle words, to babble, to prattle*." This is not faith, this is thoughtless, aimless, "*many idle words*."

Some have put forth the idea that this is contradictory to the parable that Jesus told regarding the widow who constantly petitioned the unjust judge that she might have justice from her adversary (Luke 18:1-8). She came constantly to the judge, asking for justice, asking often.

This little widow is different from the heathen. She is not babbling. She is focused. Her petition has merit and purpose. The unjust judge finally gives in because he is tired of her perseverance in the matter. Careful here. Some have said that this is what it takes for God to answer our prayers, that we must batter Him down with constant prayer to get what we need. However, Jesus says that God is not like the unjust judge, God is the Righteous Father. Jesus says, "*I tell you that He will avenge them speedily*," (Luke 18:8).

The issue of the parable is clear, Jesus tells us. "*Then He spoke a parable to them, that men always ought to pray and not lose heart*," (Luke 18:1). The heathen babbles with idle words. Christians pray in faith and purpose. We pray constantly to the Righteous Father in perseverance and trust.

The hypocrite wants to be noticed, to be seen as righteous and holy. We are called to go to our closets, to shut the doors, to commune in intimacy with the Father, our heart to His heart, our needs to His storehouse, our hurts to His love, our chaos to His peace.

The heathen prays in desperation with many idle words and babblings. He believes that he must convince God of his needs and wants, thinking He will only respond to their many words.

The Christian rests in His surrender before our righteous loving Father, knowing in faith that He will hear us speedily.

1. Most of us are familiar with the Lord's Prayer. How familiar are you with the verses just before Jesus teaches us that prayer?

_____

_____

_____

_____

2. Jesus gives us two things we should not do in prayer. The first one is the hypocrite, who wants to be seen publicly. Is there any place in you that wants or needs people to notice you in a similar fashion?

_____

_____

_____

_____

3. Do you have a secret place where you go to meet with the Lord in prayer?

_____

_____

_____

_____

4. We are also warned not to pray like heathens with many idle words and babbling. Do any of your prayers sound like this?

_____

_____

_____

_____

5. How sure are you that the Father hears your prayers?

_____

_____

_____

_____

6. In the parable of the widow and the unjust judge in Luke 18, have you ever thought of the Father as an unjust judge who did not really care about your needs?

_____

_____

_____

_____

7. At the end of that same parable, Jesus makes it clear that the Father is not like the unjust judge. That He hears us and acts speedily on our behalf. How does this change your thought process towards prayer?

_____

_____

_____

_____

8. Jesus makes it very clear in this parable that He is relating prayer to perseverance and to faith. In Luke 18:1, He says that "*men ought to pray and not lose heart.*" In the last verse of this parable (18:8) He asks another question. "*When the Son of Man comes, will He really find faith in the earth?*" How are your prayers? Are they filled with perseverance and faith?

_____

_____

_____

_____

Personal Thoughts:

Day 18: Fasting

Fasting is more than just abstaining from certain foods. Fasting is a spiritual discipline of submission and humbling ourselves toward God. It is a voluntary choice to place our attention before the Lord. In a time of great personal stress, David wrote this:

Psalm 35:13b, *"I humbled myself with fasting."*

Jesus started His personal ministry with forty days of fasting and being led by the Holy Spirit, (Matthew 4:1-2). It was said that *"Jesus returned in the power of the Spirit,"* after fasting those forty days. Why? He was not just abstaining from food; He was communing in obedience with the Holy Spirit.

Jesus gently rebuked His disciples when they were unable to cast out a demon out of an epileptic child. Jesus tied belief, faith, and power to fasting. When the disciples came and asked Jesus why they had failed, His response is interesting.

Matthew 17:20-21, *"So Jesus said to them, 'Because of your unbelief, for assuredly I say to you, if you have faith as a mustard seed, you will say to this mountain, 'Move from here to there,' and it will move; and nothing will be impossible for you.*
21 However, this kind does not go out except by prayer and fasting."

It is not just about denying our flesh and not eating. It is about humbling ourselves before the Holy Spirit of God within our lives. Fasting with prayer and the welcome acceptance of His presence through the Holy Spirit is the key to living a life of power and victory in Christ.

God addresses this in the first five verses of Isaiah 58. God says that His people have fasted improperly, attempting to use fasting to move Him toward their own desires. God rebukes their fleshly fasting. He tells them that this type of fasting is not acceptable to Him. Jesus reveals this same truth when He tells us to anoint our head with oil and not draw attention to ourselves when we fast but to turn to the Lord, (Matthew 6:17-18).

The Lord speaks about the purpose for fasting in Isaiah 58:6-

14. Perhaps these promises can bring focus to fasting in our prayers.

- To loose the bonds of wickedness.
- To undo the heavy burdens.
- To let the oppressed go free.
- To break every yoke.
- To feed the hungry, to shelter the poor and cast out, and to cover the naked.
- To confront our own flesh motives and desires.

These are the prayers that we should be praying during our fasting. Then comes the following promises of God if we do fast and pray this way:

- Our light will break forth like the morning.
- Our healing will spring forth speedily.
- Our righteousness (in Him) shall go before us.
- The glory of the Lord will be our rear guard.
- We will call out...and He will answer us.
- We will seek Him...and He will say, "*Here I am.*"
- The Lord will guide us continually.
- The Lord will satisfy our souls and strengthen us.
- We will build the old waste places.
- We will raise up the foundations of many generations.
- We will be the Repairer of the Breach and the Restorer of Streets to Dwell in.

Our fasting and prayer in humbled obedience before the Lord can change us, our families, neighborhoods, city, county, and nation. We can be a people filled with His presence and power.

As we fast together as a congregation at the beginning of this New Year, we are proclaiming that we will humbly obey and follow our Lord in submission and obedience before Him. We are experiencing in our lives the arising of faith, belief, and power that begins among us through our humble surrender to the Holy Spirit.

May we proclaim in our prayers, fasting, and lives before the Lord, "Have Your way among us Lord, have Your way."

1. How can your fasting and prayer bring a fresh humbling and submission before the Lord?

_____

_____

_____

_____

2. Jesus gave us the example of spending time with the Holy Spirit in a season of prayer and fasting? What changes might you make to welcome the Holy Spirit to meet with you and guide you?

_____

_____

_____

_____

3. Jesus' disciples were unable to cast out a demon. There is an element where our faith and belief arise in our fasting to release the power of the Holy Spirit toward His purposes. Where do you need this power? What mountains in your life need to be moved?

_____

_____

_____

_____

4. How is your fasting going? Are you just not eating? Are you also praying? What does this look like? Are you pouring the oil of His anointing over your fasting or are you sitting in sackcloth and ashes?

_____

_____

_____

_____

5. What places of bondage to wickedness in your life need to be addressed?

_____

_____

6. What places of heavy burdens, oppression, or yokes remain in your life that you need healing and freedom?

_____

_____

7. What might your life look like with His light breaking forth through you?

_____

_____

8. What does His healing look like in you mentally, spiritually, and physically?

_____

_____

9. What does His presence, righteousness, and glory around you look like?

_____

_____

10. What are some old waste places in your life and family that could be rebuilt?

_____

_____

11. How can you raise up the foundations of many generations in your family?

_____

_____

Personal Thoughts:

Day 19: Intercession

I Timothy 2:1-2, "*Therefore I exhort first of all that supplications, prayers, intercession, and giving of thanks be made for all men.*"

Paul makes a distinction in this passage between these different types of prayers. He lists four different types, supplication, prayer, intercession, and giving thanks. There must be relevant differences in these unique types of prayers.

The word in this verse for "*intercession*" is *enteuxis* (Strong's, #G1783). Here is a portion of the definition. "*a falling in with, a meeting, coming together, to visit, to converse, a conversation.*" Consider this passage.

Romans 8:34, "*Who is he who condemns? It is Christ who died, and furthermore is also risen, who is ever at the right hand of the God who also makes intercession for us.*"

The Greek word here for "*intercession*" is different, it is *entugchano* (Strong's, #G1793). It means, "*to fall in with, to go to meet a person, especially for the purpose of conversation.*" Both definitions deal with two things, proximity and conversation. Intercession is close, personal, and relational.

This is the heart of intercession. Supplications are prayers that are asking something from God. Prayers are directed at God. Prayers of thanksgiving are giving thanks and praise for what God has done. However, intercession is different. Intercession is relational. Intercession is an intentional decision to come into His presence, to visit and tarry with Him, to have a conversation. Intercession is close, personal, and intimate.

Did you notice where Jesus was at while interceding for us? He is at the right hand of the Father. He is close, He only has to turn His head to have conversation with His Father. This is the call to intercession. It is the calling to His presence. To intercede, you must know God, and He must know you.

There is something else that we find in the eighth chapter of Romans. We have just seen that Jesus makes intercession for us with the Father, but there is another who is also interceding for us with the Father.

Romans 8:26-27, *"Likewise the Spirit also helps in our weaknesses. For we do not know what we should pray for as we ought, but the Spirit Himself makes intercession for us with groanings which cannot be uttered.*
27 Now He who searches the hearts knows what the mind of the Spirit is, because He makes intercession for the saints according to the will of God."

The Holy Spirit is also making intercession for us before the Father. We don't know what to do. We don't know how to pray. We are weak, broken, confused, afraid, but the Holy Spirit intercedes on our behalf in the presence of the Father. When we had no capacity to come into the presence of the Almighty, the Holy Spirit is crying out to God concerning our weaknesses in the presence of the Father. Jesus is also there, at the right hand also interceding for us with God. The Holy Spirit is specifically interceding for us according to the perfect will of God for us.

Now it is our turn to join the Son and the Holy Spirit in the presence and throne room of God. This is the only place that true intercession can take place, and we have access to come boldly to the throne of grace because of the blood of Jesus Christ (Hebrews 4:16). The door is now open for us to come into His presence and have a conversation with our heavenly Father. This is intercession. It requires His presence and our conversing in intimacy with Him concerning His will in a situation or for a person, and whatever else we may bring before Him.

The short checklist required for intercession to take place is important. Do we know the Father? Do we have access to His presence through the blood of Christ? Are we willing to come to Him and lay our life down to talk with Him and to know His perfect will? In that place something wonderful begins to happen. Our intercession joins with the Son and with the Spirit relationally with the Father for His purpose and His will. This is intercession!

Ask the Father for your needs. Direct your prayers to Him for your situations. Give Him thanks for what He has done. Spend time in His presence interceding for His will!

1. In I Timothy chapter two, Paul gives us four different types of prayers. Supplication, prayer, intercession and giving thanks. What types of prayers do you generally pray?

_____

_____

_____

_____

2. Have you ever thought of prayer being intimate and relational with God?

_____

_____

_____

_____

3. There is a reason and a need for all four of these different types of prayers. They are needed for different situations in our lives and those that we love. Can you identify briefly where you have used each different type?

_____

_____

_____

_____

4. How does it make you feel in knowing that right now, Jesus Himself is interceding for you at the right hand of the Father?

_____

_____

_____

_____

5. Did you know that the Holy Spirit is interceding for your weaknesses and praying the perfect will of the Father over you? Does this change your thought process over your life and situations?

_____

_____

_____

_____

6. Have you ever had a conversation with God in your prayer life, or is it mostly you talking to God? Do you also take time to listen and to hear Him?

_____

_____

_____

_____

7. What might happen in your life if you begin to intentionally enter His presence and have a conversation with Him about your life, loved ones, and situations? Intimacy requires frequency, spending time often with the Lord.

_____

_____

_____

_____

8. The are just a few requirements to enter into His presence. Are you under the blood of Jesus? Are you willing to talk with the Father concerning His perfect will for your life? Are you willing to make changes according to what He says?

_____

_____

_____

_____

Personal Thoughts:

Day 20: Worship

Worship is a distinctive qualifier. Worship is a separator. Many people praise God but not all truly worship God. It has been said that you praise God for what He has done, but you worship Him because of Who He is. Here is an example.

Jesus was weary and hungry when the evil one came. Satan waited until the end of Jesus' forty days in the wilderness. He comes with offers, with a proposal. Satan offers to give Jesus all the kingdoms and glory of this world. All Jesus must do is worship him. Jesus instantly rebukes him.

Matthew 4:10, *"Then Jesus said to him, 'Away with you Satan! For it is written. 'You shall worship the Lord your God, and Him only you shall serve.'"*

There is it, the distinctive qualifier. In our lives we are to worship God and only God. People worship many different things, but to worship God means a separation from every other object of worship within our lives. That phrase *"and Him only you shall serve,"* seals that understanding. Our worship and service are to God and only to God.

The word used here in this verse for *"worship"* is *proskuneo* (Strong's #G4352). As used here the definition is, *"in the New Testament by kneeling or prostration to do homage (to one) or make obeisance, whether in order to express respect or to make supplication."* There is a word in this definition that we may not be familiar with, but it has importance for our understanding.

Obeisance means a physical action that denotes submission. This would mean bowing or prostrating before the one that we are worshipping. Often, Pastor Darrell reminds us that when we lift our hands, we are surrendering to the Lord. This is an example of obeisance.

In truth, it should be reflected in our lives, attitudes, emotions, thoughts, words, and actions. The words of our mouths should reveal our worship to God. Our actions should reveal our worship of God. Where our feet take us should reveal our worship of God. Our mind and our emotions should reveal that our life is separated in worship to Him, and only Him will we serve.

In His conversation with the woman at the well in Samaria, Jesus said this:

> **John 4:23-24**, *"But the hour is coming, and now is, when the true worshippers will worship the Father in spirit and truth; for the Father is seeking such to worship Him.*
> *24 God is Sprit, and those who worship Him must worship in spirit and truth."*

God is looking for worshippers, but not just any worshippers. There is also a distinctive qualifier in this, *"and those who worship Him must worship in spirit and truth."* Jesus says that those who do this are the *"true worshippers."*

True worshipers are real and genuine and not counterfeit or pretend. The people at church do not know our heart, but God does, and this is the separation of *"true worshippers."* God is only seeking those who will worship Him in *"spirit and truth."*

The word for *"spirit"* is *pneuma* (Strong's, #G4151). This same word is also used as the name of the Holy Spirit in the New Testament. Toward the end of the definition is this phrase, **"the disposition or influence which fills and governs the soul of any one."**

The word for *"truth"* is *aletheia* (Strong's, #G225). The relevant portion of the definition for our understanding is, **"what is true in things appertaining to God and the duties of man, moral and religious truth."** In short, this is His Word and His will.

True worshippers are men and women whose lives and spirits are filled and governed by the truths of His Word. What this means for us is that we cannot be true worshippers if we are not submitted to His truth in His Word. Unless there is obedience to His Word and His will, we cannot be true worshippers. All true worship flows out of His truth and our disposition toward it.

When the music starts, and His presence falls, we might all look the same, singing and praising, but true worshippers understand the need for obeisance. To turn every part of ourselves in submissive alignment with our God, and Him alone.

126

1. Worship is a distinctive qualifier. Worship is a separator. What does this make you think about?

_____

_____

_____

_____

2. We praise Him for what He has done; we worship Him for Who He is. Do you praise Him, or do you worship Him?

_____

_____

_____

_____

3. Jesus rebuked Satan with these words, "*You shall worship the Lord your God, and Him only you shall serve.*" Does your life reflect this truth? Are you truly serving only God?

_____

_____

_____

_____

4. Obeisance is not a word that we use much. Perhaps you have never heard of it before. Considering its definition, what does it make you think about regarding your life?

_____

_____

_____

_____

5. Jesus teaches us that the Father is looking for "*true worshippers.*" How do we know if we are a "*true worshipper?*"

_____

_____

_____

_____

6. To be a true worshiper we must worship Him in spirit. The definition for us is *"the disposition or influence which fills and governs the soul of any one."* What is the disposition of your soul? What fills and governs your inner man, your soul, thoughts, and emotions?

_____
_____
_____
_____

7. To be a true worshiper we must also worship Him in truth. The definition for us is *"what is true in things appertaining to God and the duties of man, moral and religious truth."* How does your life align with the truths of God's Word? Do you need to make changes?

_____
_____
_____
_____

Personal Thoughts:

Day 21: Declaration

Let's end our fast with a declaration. Say the following declaration out loud, and agree with God's blessing over your life and family:

Father God, I thank You for allowing me to be a part of the greatest family known to man, the family of God.

I thank you for all the benefits of being attached and grafted into the family of God.

I thank you for gifting me with the greatest gift ever given to man, the grace and mercy of Jehovah God.

Now, because I'm a believer and a child of the King, I am a recipient of His grace and mercy.

I declare today that my life and my footsteps are ordered and orchestrated by God and God alone.

I declare that His healing reigns in my body.

His provisions are available to me because I have chosen to line my life up with the precepts of God's Word.

His joy is available to me because I have chosen to put my hope and trust in the Lord.

I am not moved by what the world says, or what people say, I am moved by God's Word.

I believe that my future is in God's hand.

He is El Roi, the "God that Sees" and He sees the whole picture.

He is a rewarder of those who diligently seek Him.

Over the past 21 days I have sought Him, I have prayed, I have fasted, and I have exalted Him.

Now, because of my obedience to Him through fasting, praying, worshiping, and studying.

I, by faith, believe that there is an open heaven over my life, my family, my finances, and my church.

I declare today that the blessings of God are released to move in every area of my life.

I declare that **NO** weapon formed against me shall prosper!

I have chosen to put God first this year, and I believe that God cannot lie.

He is faithful to perform His Word in my life.

Now, I say, God I want more; More love, more grace, more mercy, more power and, most of all, more of You!

Now, I move forward this year in faith, knowing, trusting, and believing God for His absolute best in my life.

In Jesus' Name.

Final Thoughts

Congratulations! You have completed your first 21 days of prayer and fasting for this year. Our prayer is that in doing these things as the first part of the new year, it will help you establish healthy spiritual patterns for your life. Over the course of the remainder of this year, we encourage you and your family to set aside specific times and days throughout the year for prayer and fasting.

As Central Church moves now into this next year, we are so excited about what this year holds. We believe God is doing and is going to continue to do great things here at Central. Donna and I want to encourage you and your family to get involved in ministry. We believe God has placed you here to strengthen and further the kingdom with your gifts, abilities, and talents. The work that God has called us to this year will require a concentrated effort of every person. We encourage you to join our Dream Team and serve in a specific area of ministry.

You may want to get into a small group or one the many Bible studies that we offer throughout the year. There are many areas and opportunities for you to connect and serve here at Central. We believe that doing these things brings tremendous blessings and fulfillment to our lives. We truly want to see you and your family blessed in every area of life. Our prayer is that the Lord would bless you, and His face would shine upon you in every way.

We have placed a declaration in this booklet that we declare over you and your family. We encourage you to also declare this over yourself and your family on a daily basis.

As I said, in the opening of this booklet, we look forward to hearing your testimony of God's goodness and faithfulness as you move forward in obedience to Him.

Pastors Darrell and Donna Allen

About Central Church

In 2004, Pastors Darrell and Donna Allen launched Central Church with a simple mission: to lead people into a life-changing relationship with Jesus Christ.

From the beginning, Central Church has focused on reaching out to the non-churched community, building relationships with our city, and sharing the message of the Gospel.

We currently reach thousands of people, globally, each week, in person at one of our three campuses and online via livestream. We do all of this to accomplish the mission we started with.

Fasting: 21 Day Devotional is a guide for individuals to draw closer to Jesus and unite our church while we fast. We believe as we unite in prayer, fasting, and learning, we will be more effective in accomplishing our mission: to lead people into a life-changing relationship with Jesus Christ.

Made in United States
Orlando, FL
10 December 2024

55324036R00075